Original title:
Lemon Leaves and Lullabies

Copyright © 2025 Creative Arts Management OÜ
All rights reserved.

Author: Juliette Kensington
ISBN HARDBACK: 978-1-80586-390-8
ISBN PAPERBACK: 978-1-80586-862-0

Sylvan Serenades of Softness and Sweetness

In the grove where giggles grow,
A squirrel dances, putting on a show.
With acorns as hats, they prance with glee,
While birds chirp tunes for all to see.

A bumblebee buzzes, trying to sing,
But her voice is more like a buzzing fling.
She stumbles on petals and twirls in the air,
Wobbling back home with a flower to wear.

In this realm of tickles and sunny delight,
The sun slips away—oh what a sight!
Chasing shadows, a playful breeze,
Frolicking softly through whispering leaves.

Then comes the moon, with a wink and a grin,
As crickets start buzzing their nighttime din.
A raccoon in pajamas joins in the fun,
Sips on sweet dew while everyone's spun.

So gather your laughter under the stars,
Where silliness blooms and joy travels far.
In this woodland, where dreams come alive,
Every giggle and grin ensures we thrive.

Zestful Lull within the Trees

In the grove where citrus gleams,
The squirrels dance and plot their schemes.
With hats of fruit and shoes of cheer,
They sing of jams, oh, lend an ear!

A lemon tossed, it rolls away,
The birds all giggle, what a play!
With laughter bright, the breeze does sway,
Beneath the sun, we'll shout hooray!

The Restful Glow of Citrus

A calming glow in branches high,
With giggles soft, the crickets try.
They serenade with chirps and hums,
While sleepy bees don tiny drums.

A moonlit waltz, the fruit takes flight,
As owls in hats declare the night.
The tree tops sway, they're quite a sight,
In citrus dreams, all wrong feels right!

Melodies in the Scented Air

The fragrant notes, they wrap around,
With quirky sounds, what joy is found!
The raccoons hummed a silly tune,
As night descends beneath the moon.

A tangerine, a hit parade,
The citrus crew, they've come to play.
With jumpy beats and laughs to share,
In fragrant dreams, beyond compare!

Twilight Citrus Soiree

As twilight drapes the valley wide,
The laughter echoes, can't abide!
With furry friends adorned in zest,
The citrus party, truly blessed!

A silly dance, they twirl and glide,
The glow of fruit like joy applied.
With cheeky grins and hugs so tight,
The night is young; what pure delight!

Nightfall's Sweet Citrus Cradle

In the twilight, bright twists of zest,
Bouncing balls wear orange dressed.
Swaying shadows dance on walls,
While giggling fruit in laughter calls.

A sleepy bug, with jolly wing,
Plays the night like a kazoo string.
Breezes tease with tangy scents,
As dreams chase stitches of events.

Echoing Crickets and Citrus Fragrance

Crickets chirp, a fruity tune,
Underneath the quirky moon.
Laughter echoes through the glade,
Where playful thoughts in silence wade.

A puddle jumps in citrus cheer,
What a sight, oh dear, oh dear!
The fruit parade in wild delight,
Chasing shadows, taking flight.

The Lull of Orchard Spirits

Orchard sprites weave jokes with glee,
Tickling trees, oh can't you see?
Whispers frolic, nature's jest,
In the groves, they jest and rest.

A sleepy cheek, a hazy grin,
Citrus tricks that make you spin.
As stars blink down, a tasty play,
In dreams, the fruit will skip and sway.

Sun-Kissed Dreams in Yellow Haze

In the sun, with giggles bright,
Daydreams swirl in lemon light.
Chasing clouds that dance and tease,
While butterflies sail on the breeze.

Fragrant smiles in vibrant hues,
Twirling fruit, like candy temps to choose.
Whimsical limbs stretch and pose,
In a world of zesty prose.

Citrus Whispers in Twilight

Under the glow of twilight's hue,
A tangy tale begins anew.
Squeezed ideas drip like zest,
Tickling thoughts, a tiny fest.

Laughter bubbles in the air,
With citrus pranksters everywhere.
They juggle puns with nimble grace,
In the orchard's silly space.

When shadows lengthen, giggles rise,
Fruitful jokes in sunset skies.
A dancing rind upon the lawn,
As playful songs of twilight dawn.

The Sweet Scent of Slumber

In the land where fruit dreams meet,
Citrus scents twirl with sleepy feet.
Zesty naps on hammock swings,
Whispering tales of funny things.

Cuddly creatures, jolly and round,
Snore sweetly in the grassy mound.
They share their giggles in a dream,
In fruity slumbers, laughter streams.

A citrus breeze, a chuckle soft,
As silly thoughts begin to waft.
Join the snooze, let chuckles reign,
In slumber's sweet, zany domain.

Serene Citrus Dreams

Floating on a zesty cloud,
Where fruity dreams laugh out loud.
The sunbeam tickles sleepy eyes,
As giggles dance in starlit skies.

Citrus critters, warm and bright,
Crafting puns that take to flight.
From sleepy heads, ideas sprout,
In the dreamland's quirky route.

A swirl of laughter, pure delight,
In serenity, the heart takes flight.
With every chuckle, joy soared high,
In dreamy realms where fruits can sly.

Drowsy Citrus Serenade

In a grove where giggles grow,
Drowsy fruit, with zest bestowed.
A serenade of laughs and dreams,
Flowing like sweet, lively streams.

Napping gnomes with citrus hats,
Mumble jokes with sleepy chats.
They strum a tune on orange rinds,
While ticklish breezes play with minds.

The twilight hums a citrus song,
Where drowsy laughs can't be wrong.
So join the fun, let laughter swell,
In this drowsy orchard, all is well.

Gentle Chimes of Nature's Lull

When crickets sing their funny song,
A frog jumps up, it can't be wrong.
The sloths dance slow, with much delight,
Under the stars, they groove all night.

A squirrel cracks jokes with a cheeky grin,
While chasing his tail, he can't quite win.
The moon laughs softly at their prance,
As shadows join in a whimsical dance.

Twilight Hues and Citrus Rhapsody

In twilight's glow, the colors play,
A parrot raps in a colorful way.
Oranges roll down with a bounce and cheer,
As the laughing sun disappears near.

Dancing fireflies chase their own light,
While a bullfrog croaks with all its might.
The giggles of trees blend in the air,
A funny duet, nature's own flair.

Citrus Sighs Under Moonlit Skies

Under the moon, the lemons grin,
As raccoons play hide and seek to begin.
With silly puns in the night air,
Each critter laughs without a care.

A wise old owl hoots jokes of old,
While sneaky mice gather tales to be told.
Grapefruits roll like marbles in play,
As the night giggles softly away.

Blossoms of Gold and Gentle Rhymes

In a garden bright, the flowers jest,
Spouting puns, they are simply the best.
Bumblebees buzz with a tickle and tease,
With pollen confetti floating in the breeze.

A sunflower winks, trying to be sly,
As daisies chuckle beneath the sky.
The moon declares, "What a sight to see!"
While clouds join in with their fluffy glee!

Nature's Lull in Zesty Tones

In gardens bright, where fairies dance,
Tiny bugs in a merry prance.
A squirrel sneezes, oh what a sight,
Chasing shadows till the fall of night.

The flowers giggle in soft delight,
While the old tree hums with all its might.
A breeze carries whispers, a silly song,
Nature's laughter, where all belong.

Rustic Rhymes Beneath Starry Canopies

Under a sky where giggles gleam,
The owls hoot in a twilight dream.
Crickets chirp their funny tunes,
While frogs dance under the pale moons.

Stars twinkle bright, with a joking wink,
As fireflies plot and start to think.
A raccoon stirs the pot, what a mess,
In this rustic world, chaos is blessed.

Harmonious Notes of a Whimsical Orchard

In orchards where laughter spills like juice,
Apples bay for a good excuse.
Pigs in overalls, laughing with flair,
Trying to dance, but none seem to care.

The wind teases peaches, saying, "Don't pout!"
While cherries giggle, spinning about.
A guitar made of twigs strums away,
As funny fruit sing through the day.

Evening Melodies in Citrus Hues

As dusk settles with a zesty sigh,
A chubby raccoon waves goodbye.
Lemons grumble about their tart fate,
While oranges laugh, feeling quite great.

The night brings wit from feathered friends,
As crickets play tunes, the fun never ends.
The moon smirks softly, a glow in the air,
Winking at shadows that dance everywhere.

Sweet Escape of Spring Nights

Bouncing dreams on a warm breeze,
Laughter hides beneath the trees.
Tree frogs croak in a jazz-like tone,
While sugar ants march, never alone.

Fireflies dance in a sparkly flight,
Their tiny lights bring the dark delight.
A raccoon tips his cap with flair,
Winking at stars without a care.

Pajamas and giggles fill the air,
With soda cans shaking without a dare.
The moon grins like a fountain of cheer,
As whispers of spring bloom soft and clear.

Dreams in Tangy Pastels

Pastel skies with a citrus glint,
Silly stories and wild hints.
Kites fly high, in pirouetting swirls,
Chasing rainbows and twirling pearls.

A piñata hung from an old swing tree,
With gummy worms that giggle with glee.
In the corner, a kid shares a joke,
While laughter erupts in a zesty smoke.

Sipping breezes in mugs held tight,
Each joke launches like a rocket in flight.
These moments bubble up like seltzer sweet,
In the laughter-tinted land where friends meet.

Dusky Hues of Citrus Tranquility

Sunset hues blend with the laugh of night,
Giggles ripple, oh what a sight.
Whiskers twitch on the hippo's face,
As kids chase fireflies in a playful race.

Soft shadows play tag with half-moon light,
A clown fish juggles dreams so bright.
The kitty cat hums a jazz refrain,
While the crickets tap dance on windowpane.

Clouds become cushions, so fluffy and round,
Resting in layers without a sound.
With every chuckle, the evening glows,
Painting the night with whimsy that flows.

Harmonies of the Evening Fruit

Underneath a berry-laden tree,
Chattering monkeys swing with glee.
The giant peach whispers a funny tale,
Of a snail that dreamed to set sail.

Tangerine giggles rush through the air,
As laughter twirls with whimsical flair.
Bananas sing songs of silly things,
While laughter stretches just like springs.

The night wraps us in a cotton candy coat,
As fireflies join in a glowing boat.
Every joke a sprinkle, every smile a treat,
In a world where silliness creates the beat.

Swaying Branches and Serene Songs

In the breeze, they dance so light,
Branches giggle, oh what a sight.
Swinging low, swaying high,
Caught a branch, and waved goodbye.

Boughs that chuckle, thick and bright,
Yelling health on sunny nights.
Fruits above hang with a sway,
Whispering tales of the day.

Laughter echoes through the grove,
The wind's a friend, the trees approve.
A twist, a turn, a playful spin,
Join the fun, let the games begin!

Notes float down like butterflies,
Singing tunes that provoke surprise.
Joyful beats the roots do share,
In this grove, you find your care.

Garden of Sweet Scented Whispers

A garden blooms with flavors bold,
Whispers wander, stories told.
Petals laughing, scents arise,
Tickling noses with surprise.

Giggling buds upon the trail,
Each twist and turn tells a tale.
Sassy scents that prance and play,
Chasing worries far away.

Sunbeams shine like golden cheese,
Bees are buzzing, what a tease!
Swirling scents in sunny patches,
Garden gags that come with hatches.

Nectar drips from joyful blooms,
Gathering sweetened, fragrant fumes.
Citrus jokes abound with cheer,
In this garden, joy is near.

Nostalgia in Every Zestful Note

Remember when we'd slice the fruit,
Laughter spilling, who could dispute?
Zesty bites, a party cheer,
Memories swell, always near.

Citrus laughter fills the air,
Dancing to tunes beyond compare.
A wink, a grin, with every slice,
Nostalgia poured like syrup, nice.

Jams and jests in jars we keep,
Hidden treasures, laughs so deep.
Notes that swell with zingy glee,
Drawing smiles from you and me.

Each foray down memory lane,
Uncorking joy, not a drop of pain.
Sipping songs, fresh and bright,
In every note, we find the light.

Mild Murmurs of Citrus Kisses

In the sun, we share a laugh,
Citrus whispers, the perfect half.
Breezes tickle, giggles bloom,
Around the tree, we dance and zoom.

Sour notes and sweet delight,
Playfully mingling, pure and bright.
Tasting joy in every peel,
A happy harvest, what a deal!

Murmurs rise in gentle waves,
Tickling toes, the heart behaves.
Citrus kisses float on air,
Wrapping warmth, a tender care.

A sunny smile, a joyous song,
In this moment, we belong.
Mild and merry, night will gleam,
The world's a canvas, burst with dream.

Whispered Hints of Summer

In the garden, mischief flows,
Tiny critters in funny rows.
Sunshine tickles, bright and warm,
Nature's antics, a playful swarm.

Birds wear sunglasses, chirp and sway,
Caterpillars dance, trying to play.
With wobbly steps, the ants parade,
A silly spectacle, nature's charade.

Dreams Infused with Citrus Gold

A fuzzy bee with mismatched socks,
Buzzes near the tickling docks.
Lemons giggle in the breeze,
Thoughts of lemonade bring us to tease.

Sipping nectar, hoot and howl,
Fruit bats play, each wearing a towel.
Winks exchanged in a zesty glow,
Summer tales that twist and flow.

Twilight's Citrus Cauldron

Under twilight, bugs in a rush,
Fireflies debate in a buzzy hush.
Silly shadows waltz on the ground,
Whiskers twitching, laughter unbound.

Toads sport hats, frogs croak a tune,
While crickets dance to the light of the moon.
In a pot, the night brews fun,
Squeezed sunshine under stars, we run.

Melody of the Golden Orchard

In the orchard, giggles abound,
Citrus scents dance all around.
Fruits with faces hold a fair,
Making jokes, a fruity affair.

Apples sing and pears play tag,
While oranges gossip and fruit flies brag.
With every chuckle, sweetness grows,
In this orchard, laughter flows.

Midnight Citrus Reveries

In the moonlight, oranges dance,
While lemons giggle in a trance.
Peels slip under sleepy feet,
Sour jokes make the night so sweet.

Crickets chirp a citrus song,
Mice wear hats, and play along.
Sassy fruits sway with delight,
As shadows join the silly flight.

The night is ripe with zestful cheer,
Chasing dreams of fruity beer.
A bouncing branch, a giggling tree,
Teases those who dare to see.

And when dawn breaks, laughter fades,
Yet hints of zest still serenade.
A sleepy sun gives a bright grin,
While citrus dreams start to begin.

The Gentle Breeze and Golden Glow

A breeze so soft, it tickles ears,
Splits the gloom and stirs up cheers.
Golden rays, they frolic and play,
The garden's stage for a bright ballet.

Green buds blush, their colors bright,
Swapping secrets in the light.
A tangerine winks with glee,
As bees whisper, "Come dance with me!"

Saucy lemons roll and slide,
In zany backflips, they take pride.
Their punchlines land with a happy thud,
Sending giggles in a citrus flood.

When evening falls, the laughter hums,
To the rhythm of playful drums.
Stars appear, a cheeky show,
As night wears its fruity glow.

Citrus Caress in the Quiet

Under hush of a whispering tree,
A quirky fruit party starts with glee.
Limes lounge past the twinkle lights,
While grapefruit jokes take eager flights.

Soft feathers from the pillows dance,
Hosting a sweet, bubbly chance.
Lemons giggle, oh what fun!
As shadows tumble one by one.

A zesty breeze stirs the calm,
With a hint of a citrus balm.
Nearby a cricket tries a line,
A punchline ripe, oh so divine!

In the quiet, laughter binds,
As sleepy fruits share their finds.
A gentle hug from the night sky,
Cradles laughter as dreams flit by.

Lullabies of the Orchard

Underneath the twinkling stars,
Orchard critters strum guitars.
A serenade of citrus tones,
As mischief stirs amidst the stones.

Sweet nectar drips, the frogs all croon,
In harmony with the sleepy moon.
Peach pits tap their tiny feet,
Creating rhythms bitter-sweet.

With every strum, a giggle grows,
As dancing fruit parade in rows.
Pineapples spin with joyful zest,
While oranges joke, "We're the best!"

As night deepens with playful sighs,
The orchard roars with fruity lies.
In this lullaby of blissful cheer,
The playful orchard hums, "We're here!"

Nurtured by Nature's Lull

In a garden where giggles bloom,
Butterfly prances, avoiding the broom.
Sunshine tickles the petals bright,
Nature's antics guide us to light.

Frogs croak jokes beneath the moon,
Silly tales float, like a hot air balloon.
Swaying trees sing songs of cheer,
With each rustle, laughter draws near.

Bumblebees buzz, crafting delight,
Catch them dancing in sheer moonlight.
Ladybugs join, sporting a bow,
In this merry garden, joy's sure to grow.

Peaceful Murmurs under the Stars

Stars giggle softly above so bright,
Winking and twinkling with all their might.
Crickets chirp with a pinch of sass,
Whispering secrets that come to pass.

Clouds drift gently with a playful nudge,
As fireflies dart like bright little buds.
Night wraps the world in a cozy hug,
While shadows dance on that comfy rug.

Moonbeams tease and join the fun,
Lighting pathways for everyone.
Under this blanket of cosmic glee,
Nature hums soft, a whimsical spree.

Citrus-Cloaked Tranquility

Lemons roll down the sunny lane,
Laughing at puns, feeling no pain.
Orange socks on a butterfly's feet,
Skatering grooves to a playful beat.

Giggling fruits plan a sweet parade,
As zestful whispers begin to invade.
With every twist and every funk,
The garden blooms with a jolly clunk.

A cat in shades sings the blues,
As citrus scents paint happy hues.
In this circus of fruits, we find,
Joy woven sweetly, wonderfully kind.

Serenades in Twilight's Embrace

Twilight wraps its arms so wide,
While fireflies twirl and daringly glide.
Singing crickets host a nightly show,
With offbeat rhythms that steal the glow.

A raccoon wearing a top hat spins,
Dancing circles with wobbling grins.
Mice in tuxedos join the delight,
As stars peek in, chuckling at night.

Life's a banquet, chaos galore,
With chocolate rivers and a citrus shore.
In twilight's embrace, we're all the same,
Joking and laughing, igniting the flame.

Cozy Citrus Nook of Dreams

In a nook where the fruit hangs bright,
Cats chase shadows, giggling at night.
Sippers of juice make cheers and clinks,
While squirrels do dances, as everyone thinks.

Lemonade rivers, sweet and sour,
Bouncing along like a cheerful flower.
Giggling children in the warm glow,
Launch silly jokes as they twirl to and fro.

Fireflies blink like little lights,
As frogs croak rhythm in soft moonlit nights.
The fun never ends in this fruity space,
Where dreams and laughter color the place.

Tangy Tides of Nightfall

The sun dips low in a zestful swirl,
Tickling the waves with a citrus twirl.
A jolly breeze whispers tales untold,
Of gummy bears dancing, all brave and bold.

Chickens in aprons, baking quite high,
Making pie crusts that seem to fly.
Citrus pies atop roller skates,
Rolling downhill, oh, the funny fates!

Nights full of giggles, music so sweet,
Juggling lemons and toe-tapping feet.
Join in the chaos, embrace the cheer,
For this juicy riot brings everyone near.

Whispers of Citrus Nights

A breeze brings whispers of zesty delight,
As squirrels recite poems under moonlight.
Giggling ghosts in a citrusy park,
Share funny secrets that spark in the dark.

Yellow balloons launch into the sky,
While tangerine fairies flit and fly.
Dancing on clouds, they twirl without rest,
Making funny faces, oh, how they jest!

The laughter echoes, a citrusy song,
As the night stretches, holding us strong.
With every burst of sunshine and fun,
A whimsical world where we all run.

Melodies in a Garden's Embrace

In a garden where giggles bloom,
Citrus fruits sway, dispelling all gloom.
Bouncing bunnies with hats askew,
Singing lullabies in orange and blue.

A caterpillar strums a tiny guitar,
While ladybugs dance in a wild bazaar.
Swinging on petals, they laugh with glee,
Sharing sweet tales from the old citrus tree.

The moon peers in with a quirky smile,
As frogs in tuxedos croak with style.
In this garden of fun, with dreams that race,
Every moment blooms with laughter and grace.

Zesty Dreams of Night

In the land where citrus gleams,
Silly whispers flow like streams,
A giggle here and laughter there,
Bouncing like a fluffy flare.

Under stars with zest we play,
Chasing dreams that bounce away,
With every twist and silly cheer,
We dance around, without a fear.

A citrus twist upon our sleep,
Jokes so funny, they're ours to keep,
A friendly breeze brings forth a tease,
And cuddles wrapped in citrus ease.

Aromas in the Moonlight

Moonbeams sprinkle on the grass,
As we giggle, letting time pass,
The scent of fun fills the air,
We twirl around, without a care.

Laughter bounces, soft and sweet,
With every note, we tap our feet,
The night sings songs of silly dreams,
In fragrant whirls and playful beams.

We skip through shadows, light as air,
Making faces, stripping despair,
A gentle breeze, a playful sigh,
As aromas dance and dreams fly high.

Tangy Nights and Soft Melodies

The stars are glowing, bold and bright,
While we crack jokes in pure delight,
With tangy tales from dusk till dawn,
We giggle 'til the yawns are drawn.

Each soft melody whispers low,
As silly shenanigans start to flow,
Twists of fate, oh what a trip,
With every laugh, we take a sip.

In the dance of dreams, we collide,
With tangy humor, we can't hide,
The night is ours, so full of cheer,
As we spin 'round and shed a tear.

The Slumbering Grove

In a grove where light-hearted plays,
Dreams take form in flicker and sway,
With quirky sounds, the night awakes,
And sleepy giggles fill the lakes.

Beneath the branches, breezy and fine,
We joke about the stars that shine,
Each whisper floats like citrus mist,
In this soft night, none can resist.

With cozy hugs and playful tease,
In tangled dreams, we find our ease,
Soft melodies cradle our sleepy heads,
In the grove, where laughter spreads.

Soft Shadows of Orchard Dreams

In the grove where sunlight gleams,
The squirrels plot their nutty schemes.
A dance of shadows, oh so spry,
They leap and bound, then wave goodbye.

Bouncing bees take flight with cheer,
Wearing tiny hats, it's clear.
They buzz a tune, they swirl, they dive,
To spontaneous jams, they come alive.

Beneath the trees, a picnic laid,
With cucumber sandwiches, neatly displayed.
A cheeky fox steals a crumb, it seems,
And everyone giggles in orchard dreams.

As twilight whispers, night descends,
The owls hoot, and laughter blends.
A nightcap made of fresh-squeezed glee,
In the orchard's heart, we're wild and free.

Harmonies of Sunlight and Green

In patches of grass where giggles play,
The ants have staged a ballet today.
They twirl on blades, in colorful flair,
Taking their bows like they just don't care.

A chubby rabbit hops in time,
His rhythm might not be sublime.
But everyone claps in joyful refrain,
For bunnies can dance without any shame.

With lemonade spills, the kids all scream,
Like sticky sweet splashes from a dream.
They race and tumble, the sun's warm spin,
In this green kingdom, we all win!

The sun dips low, the shadows grow tall,
While fireflies join in the twilight ball.
We wave our hands, the night takes flight,
In harmonies bright under the moonlight.

The Cradle of Scented Breezes

In gardens filled with fragrant cheer,
The scents of blooming flowers appear.
Butterflies in ties, they flutter around,
In a whimsical world where joy is found.

A sneaky snail with a shell so grand,
Embarks on a journey across the land.
He leaves a trail of giggles behind,
While his slow-paced dance is full of grind.

With every breeze, a ticklish tease,
The flowers sway like a happy breeze.
And petals tangle in hair so wild,
As laughter rings out, a spirit reviled.

The sun dips down, the colors merge,
A tumble of whispers like a playful surge.
In the cradle of scents, we drift and sway,
As sleep serenades us at the end of play.

Echoes of Citrus Serenade

In the orchard where zesty dreams bloom,
The fruit sings sweetly, dispelling gloom.
A trio of birds in a citrus trees sway,
With notes that dance and tumble away.

A playful breeze, it twirls through the land,
Tickling cheeks, it's perfectly planned.
With citrus slices, oh so bright,
A feast of laughter in the fading light.

The shadows stretch as twilight descends,
And the fireflies start to make amends.
We sip on cheer, as stories unfold,
In echoes of joy, both brave and bold.

When stars arrive, the laughter lingers,
Like twinkling notes on fluttering fingers.
In this serenade of the night and day,
We dance with happiness, come what may.

Lull of the Grove

In a twist of sun and shade,
Grove critters plan a parade.
Squirrels toss and raccoons glide,
While the frogs river dance side by side.

Bees hum tunes of sugary dreams,
As chipmunks giggle by the streams.
A breeze whispers through the trees,
Inviting all to join with ease.

But wait, a banana peel's out!
One little slip brings a loud shout.
Everyone tumbles, rolls, and laughs,
While nature snaps a thousand photos for its crafts.

So come and join this silly dance,
With every rhythm, feel the chance.
For when the sun begins to set,
The grove's sweet laughter's the best bet.

Nightfall's Tangy Embrace

As stars twinkle in a fruity glow,
A raccoon tells jokes, putting on a show.
Owls snicker at a jumping gnome,
While fireflies flash, lighting up the dome.

A grapefruit moon starts to grin bright,
Soft giggles echo in the soft night.
A pickle on a stick? It's quite the sight!
Everyone wonders who took the bite.

With each giggle, the shadows sway,
Beneath the stars, they twirl and play.
In this zesty night, joy won't cease,
As giggling creatures find their peace.

So when you think of fun and cheer,
Just remember the antics, loud and clear.
For in the night, under the playful light,
Every silly tale brings delight.

Sleepy Citrus Crescendo

In a sleepy orchard, dreams unfold,
Where fruits wear pajamas, all cozy and bold.
Juicy oranges start to snore,
While berries giggle, shouting, "More!"

The lemon tree starts to sway,
Sending sleepy whispers our way.
Grapes yawn wide, stretching their stems,
In this slumber party of fruity gems.

Then a cheeky lime rolls off in a dash,
Giggling, he makes quite the splash.
Sleepy heads turn, eyes open wide,
As all the fruit get swept in the tide.

So snuggle close, dear fruity friends,
With laughter and dreams, this fun never ends.
In this sleepy crescendo, take your rest,
For when morning comes, we will jest!

Golden Zest and Gentle Hues

One fine day in a cheerful patch,
The fruits played hide-and-seek, a fun match.
Pineapples chuckled, hiding in the grass,
While peaches blushed as the minutes pass.

Then a tangerine giggled, hopping high,
In his zestful dance, reaching the sky.
Golden hues shimmer, all bright and round,
As laughter echoes through the ground.

A playful scribbler, a lemony sprite,
Draws silly faces in the fading light.
With fruity crowns, they dance and spin,
In a world where silliness wins the win.

So come and join this fruity fest,
With giggles and zests, you'll feel blessed.
For when the day wraps in gentle hues,
Every laugh is the best kind of muse.

Calm Echoes from an Orchard's Heart

In the orchard, a giggle goes,
Where the fruit wears a sun-kissed pose.
The branches sway in merry prance,
Inviting fresh thoughts to dance.

A squirrel dons a fruit hat tight,
Offering snacks in sheer delight.
As bees buzz with a cheeky hum,
Nature's chorus makes all hearts drum.

A breeze tickles the leaves so green,
Whispering secrets, a playful scene.
The sun winks on a daffodil,
While shadows frolic, hearts to fill.

Fruits giggle as they share a jest,
In this kingdom, they all feel blessed.
And all around, the joy swells high,
As laughter lights the azure sky.

Crescendos of Citrus Starlight

Under twinkling stars so bright,
Oranges chat till the morning light.
A lemon slips on a peppy tune,
While grapefruits dance 'neath the silvery moon.

Frogs croak as they keep the beat,
While the tangerines elegantly meet.
They sway with cheeky twirls and spins,
As laughter bursts, the fun begins.

A cat in a hat joins the affair,
Chasing shadows without a care.
With every leap, a joke is tossed,
These citrus friends know no cost.

The night is filled with laughter's cheer,
In this orchard, worries disappear.
With each sweet note, the world exists,
In this fruity realm, we can't resist.

Serene Shadows of Fragrant Moments

In soft shadows where the fruits play,
Time rolls gently, come what may.
Bananas tell tales of silly quests,
While berries laugh like jesting guests.

A napping snail with dreams so grand,
Draws funny maps across the land.
Grapes gossip from their twining vine,
Sharing jokes that taste divine.

The sun drips golden, light so free,
Tickling petals on every tree.
In this haven, the fruit parade,
Makes each worry swiftly fade.

A chirping bird with a curious glance,
Sings of whimsy in a fanciful dance.
In fragrant moments, laughter's sound,
Creates a joy that knows no bound.

Whispers of Green in Twilight's Embrace

When twilight hugs the happy leaves,
Citrus secrets are what it weaves.
A dancing sprite with zestful flair,
Unleashes laughter, light as air.

The mushrooms chuckle, soaking rays,
Inviting all to game-filled days.
Feisty fairies join in the spree,
As nature's humor flows like a sea.

Fruits trade jokes with a wink and grin,
Plotting mischief as night draws in.
As shadows stretch into playful leaps,
Even the stars join, winks and peeps.

In every whisper of the breeze,
Humor blooms among the trees.
So let your heart, in laughter, sway,
Embracing peace at the end of day.

The Lifting of a Golden Yawn

In the morning, sunbeams play,
Bouncing bright, they chase dreams away.
A fluffy cat sprawls on the bed,
Chasing shadows in her sleepy head.

The toast pops up, it's dancing joy,
While the kettle gives a steamy ploy.
With mismatched socks, I take a stand,
Is this chaos, or a fun-filled land?

A mug of cheer, it starts to sing,
Sugar-swirls make the heart take wing.
Butterflies flit with a goofy grin,
As breakfast giggles, let the fun begin!

A golden yawn stretches wide,
In the zany world, I'll take my ride.
In a bubble of laughter, I'll stay afloat,
With every chuckle, the day's antidote.

Slumber's Zesty Refuge

In a cozy nook, where dreams collide,
Sleepy treasures, my secret hide.
A tangerine cat with paws so small,
Whiskers twitch, as she gives it her all.

With pillows piled high, like fluffy hills,
And a snore that shakes the windowsills.
Snuggled tight under blankets bright,
I giggle softly at the morning light.

Chasing the day with a wink and a grin,
A fruit basket spills, let the snacking begin!
Citrus dreams dance on the ceiling,
While sleep's comical tunes are revealing.

Here in this haven, where fun is king,
Every bubble of sleep just makes my heart swing.
With zest in my dreams and laughter on cue,
I'll wake up quite silly, maybe even in blue!

Whispered Peace in the Orchard

In the orchard where giggles bloom,
The air is tart with citrus perfume.
A squirrel prances, quite smug and spry,
Stealing fruits with a mischievous eye.

Beneath the branches, where shadows play,
A wiggly worm starts to sway.
With a dance so silly, it steals the show,
While birds chirp notes in a rowdy flow.

Amidst the laughter, a breeze softly sighs,
As babbling streams join the butterflies.
The sun hangs low, in a pastel scene,
Where whispers of fun make the heart feel keen.

So let's frolic 'neath the fruity crowns,
While jesters in trees wear leafy gowns.
In this cheery place, we sing and sway,
With each chuckle, we chase the gray.

Cocoa Star and Citrus Moon

When the cocoa star winks from the sky,
And the citrus moon gives a gentle sigh,
I sit on the porch, a snack in hand,
Dreaming of worlds so perfectly planned.

Pajama-clad squirrels race on by,
As night laughs softly, oh my, oh my!
With chocolate beams and orange zest glow,
The absurdity tickles my toes below.

Cupcakes in orbit, the stars tease each night,
While lemony giggles lead flights of delight.
As the cocoa swirls and the moon starts to grin,
I'll dance with the shadows until dreams begin.

So let's toast to the night, in a silly renown,
With an orchard of laughter in this twilight town.
The cocoa star winks; the citrus moon beams,
In this whimsical life, we'll weave our dreams.

The Peaceful Orchard

In a grove where giggles grow,
Fruits whisper secrets, don't you know?
Chasing bugs with berry pies,
Laughter blooms beneath the skies.

Squirrels read their acorn books,
While a raccoon steals the cooks.
Grumpy owls in plaid pajamas,
Swapping tales like old grandmamas.

Every breeze a gentle tease,
As the rabbits dance with ease.
Butterflies in polka dots,
Make the veg a starlit spot.

And in this smiley orchard land,
The bees hum sweetly, look, just stand!
For here, beneath the sun's delight,
All is merry, all is bright.

Whispers of the Nurtured Grove

In a wood where shadows smile,
Critters frolic all the while.
Snakes in bowties, turtles waltzing,
Making mischief, quite exhausting.

The foxes paint in vibrant hues,
While owls share their snooze reviews.
Each twig bends with laughter's song,
Nature's jokes, they can't go wrong.

A squirrel wears a tiny hat,
While acorns bounce off a sleepy cat.
Here, the trees tell tales anew,
Of a mischievous motley crew.

So come and dance, don't hesitate,
In the grove, it's never late.
With whispers spun in playful spirit,
Join the fun; you'll surely hear it!

Soft Citrus Tides

At the edge where fruits all dip,
The lemons play a citrus quip.
Oranges sing in sunny tones,
While grapefruits tell silly groans.

Watermelons roll and sway,
As the juicers join the play.
Citrus waves, oh what a sight,
Splashing joy with all their might.

In this tide of zesty cheer,
Lemons juggle, no hint of fear.
Tangerines on surfboards glide,
As the zestful songs collide.

So let the sunny laughter ring,
For here, the fruits can truly sing.
In this soft and silly mirth,
Citrus friends know true rebirth.

Hush of the Fruited Night

When stars come out to dance and gleam,
The fruits get ready for their dream.
Couches made of cherry vines,
Cantaloupes with cozy lines.

But here in the night, squirrels crack jokes,
As oranges tease the sleepy folks.
Each lemon laughs, a gleeful plight,
In a hush, they share their light.

Moonlit nights bring tales of fun,
As sleepy fruits count one by one.
Walnuts play the gentle drums,
While the whole grove quietly hums.

So find your place beneath this tree,
Where fruity dreams are wild and free.
In the hush of night's embrace,
All is silly, all is grace.

Dappled Shadows and Sweet Hush

In the orchard where giggles play,
Trees sway gently, come what may.
A cat in a hat, what a sight!
Chasing dreams on this moonlit night.

A chorus of crickets join in the dance,
With a skip and a hop, they take a chance.
Frogs wear tuxedos, oh what a mash!
While fireflies twinkle, creating a splash.

Under the stars, a party of fun,
Whispers of secrets 'til morning's begun.
Oranges juggle, lemons tease,
A tickle of laughter carried in the breeze.

So come take a stroll through this sweet place,
Where whimsy and joy fill every space.
Join in the frolic, let your heart soar,
In dappled shadows, we laugh evermore!

Night's Citrus Tint

Moonlight spills like juice in a glass,
Where critters collide in a whimsical class.
A squirrel in slippers, oh what a sight,
Doing the cha-cha under the starlight.

The stew of the garden's nightly charm,
With giggles bubbling, all cozy and warm.
Grapefruits gossip, tangy and bright,
While snickering shadows playfully fight.

Fireflies waltz with the softest of grace,
The mischief of mirrors puts smiles on every face.
Laughter drizzles like syrup on pies,
As the silly critters spin under the skies.

So raise a toast to this funny parade,
In the citrus glow where memories are made.
With every chuckle tucked in your heart,
Let the serenade of silliness start!

Serenade of Soft Citrus Starlight

With a hop, skip, and a playful cheer,
The silliness of fruit brings joy near.
Bouncing bananas sing a tune,
While giggling pumpkins dance 'neath the moon.

Lemons toss jokes like sweet confetti,
While nutty squirrels get all too sweaty.
They trip and tumble in pure delight,
Creating a ruckus through the soft night.

A chorus of giggles floats on the breeze,
As oranges juggle with utmost ease.
Each quirky critter plays their sweet part,
In this nighttime concert that tickles the heart.

So let's join the fun, just you and I,
Under the blanket of the twinkling sky.
With laughter and light in this fruity expanse,
We'll waltz with the stars in a silly dance!

Moonlit Whispers of the Orchard

In the hush of night, the orchard awakes,
With whispers of whimsy, the earth gently quakes.
A rambunctious rabbit, quite dressed to impress,
Twirls in a dance, a true moonlit mess.

The trees all chuckle, their branches a sway,
As zestful critters come out to play.
Citrus smiles spread across the ground,
While chortles and giggles in harmony sound.

A merry-go-round of fruits in bright hues,
Twisting and turning, gossiping their cues.
Pineapples wear crowns with a regal air,
While lemons laugh loud without a care.

So join the parade 'neath the shimmering light,
With frolicsome friends, it feels so right.
In this orchard of laughter, let worries be few,
As moonlit whispers share joy just for you!

A Tinge of Tang in Stillness

In a garden bright and zesty,
A squirrel tried to dance all testy.
He slipped on skins, oh what a sight,
His dance now turned to quite a fright.

The moonlight laughed, a chuckle soft,
While crickets played their tunes aloft.
The air was sweet with hints of zest,
A comedy show, nature's best.

With every bounce, a giggle flew,
As birds joined in, a feathery crew.
They sang of mishaps, tails askew,
A playful serenade, so true.

And so on through the silent night,
The garden whispered laughs in flight.
Each rustle brought a silly tease,
As laughter danced upon the breeze.

The Quiet Melodies of Night

A cat with flair, so sly and spry,
Decided it was time to fly.
He leapt for stars, but caught a tree,
The rustling leaves laughed merrily.

The owls hooted in surprise,
At furry antics 'neath the skies.
A nighttime concert, bright and bold,
With stories of adventures told.

A sneaky mouse, with cheese in tow,
He tiptoed past, quite proud, you know!
The cat, now stuck, with laughter shared,
Became the night's most honored bard.

And while the moon spun tales of old,
The universe rolled with laughter untold.
It's funny how the stars would gleam,
When nighttime plays out like a dream.

Citrus Dreams take Flight

In a grove where shadows play,
A bird forgot the words to say.
He chirped a tune, quite out of line,
The trees just swayed, their laughter fine.

With wings so bright and sunshine cheer,
He tried to sing, but not so clear.
The bees would buzz, but had to grin,
As petals twirled and joined him in.

A branch gave way, and down he went,
Crashing into blossoms, quite content.
The flowers giggled, petals twirled,
A citrus circus, joy unfurled.

As dreams took flight in silly ways,
The skies erupted, bright in plays.
The dance of nature, far from strife,
Is where we find our laugh-filled life.

Savoring Night's Gentle Touch

A raccoon in the pantry pranced,
He thought at night, he'd found romance.
But jars of jam proved quite a foe,
And led him on a tweedle-dee show.

He tumbled 'round in jelly's grip,
A sticky fingered, sad old trip.
The nightstand lamp began to sway,
As laughter peeped, "Oh, not today!"

Outside, the stars wore grins so wide,
As crickets watched, their eyes open wide.
Each crash and thud held songs of cheer,
In pantry chaos, joy drew near.

The moon inspired a laughing glance,
Impromptu fun, the raccoon's dance.
As night held tight its gentle clutch,
We find our sweetness in the touch.

Nighttime Reflections in Green

The moon hangs low, quite round and bright,
A frog croaks loud, causing a fright.
Crickets chirp in a silly song,
While fireflies dance, where we belong.

Leaves rustle softly, a shy little breeze,
Whispers of secrets from the tall trees.
A raccoon in pajamas gets caught in a stare,
Wondering how he got there without a care.

Stars peek out, like children at play,
Laughing and hiding, they gleefully sway.
The night's a circus, no need for the light,
Under a blanket of laughter, we dream tonight.

Solstice Sounds Beneath the Trees

Squirrels hold concerts, drumming with glee,
Raccoons are the band, as wild as can be.
A singing grasshopper steals the show,
While a wise old owl watches below.

The sun sets low, the warmth fades away,
But the laughter of animals stays for the day.
Crickets take center, with a spotlight on stage,
While shadows join in, a curious rage.

Rustling of leaves, a comedic ballet,
The forest is giggling, oh what a display!
With every twist and turn, the fun never ends,
In nature's own theater, where all are friends.

Gentle Hush of Citrus Breezes

A breeze flutters in, with a citrusy grin,
Tickling the leaves, where the fun will begin.
The odd little worms join in on the score,
While ants march along, a parade to adore.

Whispers of laughter, from branches above,
As ladybugs gossip, as if they're in love.
Bees do the cha-cha, buzzing with flair,
While butterflies giggle and dance in the air.

A colorful mishap, a fruit roll away,
Causing a frenzy, oh what a display!
In this merry garden, we chuckle and sway,
Where nature's a joke, every single day.

Rhythms of Nature's Golden Glow

The sun rises up, like a jester on stage,
Painting the world in a bright yellow page.
Flowers are laughing, their petals all bright,
As bees stumble over, in their dizzy flight.

A caterpillar wobbles, in a dance most absurd,
While butterflies snicker, their wings gently stirred.
Trees sway with laughter, a humorous show,
Bending and bowing, putting on a glow.

The stream bubbles over, tales to unfold,
With frogs as the narrators, as stories are told.
Nature's a circus, with everyone in line,
In rhythms of joy, where happiness shines.

Murmurs from the Citrus Orchard

In a grove where whispers play,
The fruits toss secrets all the day.
A squirrel steals a citrus grin,
While bees debate where fun begins.

The branches sway, they have a chat,
About the cat who wore a hat.
The sun joins in with playful rays,
As oranges chuckle in the blaze.

A parrot yells, "Get off my turf!"
While frogs compose their silly slurf.
The breeze just giggles, passing by,
With juicy jokes that make you sigh.

And when the night descends with flair,
The fruit holds hands, with zest to share.
With stars above, they start to hum,
In this orchard, joy's never numb.

The Calm Before the Blossom

Before the blooms could stretch and yawn,
The dandelions dance at dawn.
A snail in boots, quite out of shape,
Wanders slowly, mischief drape.

The sun peeks through with a cheesy grin,
While worms prepare for a wiggly spin.
The ladybugs plan a feathery dive,
In shades of green, they come alive.

A tiny ant slips on a twig,
And lets out a laugh, feeling big.
The morning air, a songbird's cheer,
With jokes that tickle all who hear.

And just before the petals burst,
The whole grove giggles, it's truly cursed!
For in this dance, not one is shy,
Each twist and twirl always brings a sigh.

Dreaming in Citrus Shades

In shadows soft, a tangerine day,
The fruit flies giggle, oh what play!
They plot to steal a lemon's hat,
While crickets chirp, and sleep brings that.

A butterfly twirls on its way,
With colors bright, a bold display.
And in the breeze, a cheeky sprite,
Jumps in and out, playing all night.

An orange twirls upon a vine,
Singing softly, 'Life is fine!'
While shadows break into a run,
Chasing echoes, just for fun.

And when the moon starts peeking through,
The stars all giggle, feeling new.
In dreamy hues, they fade and blend,
In citrus spells, all troubles mend.

Soft Hues of Evening

As twilight drips on golden hue,
The fruits all gather, a lively crew.
A peach tells tales of the day's fun,
While crickets tune their evening run.

The pears perform a dance of cheer,
While wobbly grapefruits draw them near.
Each bough shakes with laughter bright,
As stars awaken in their light.

The moon gives whispers, soft and round,
As fruits all giggle, joy unbound.
In the orchard's heart, a friendship grows,
In chuckles shared, hilarity glows.

So raise a glass, the juice is sweet,
For every pomelo brings a beat.
In this evening's hush, we find delight,
With merry friends, we dance through the night.

Peace Echoes in Fruity Bliss

In a garden of smiles, bright and sweet,
Laughter twirls with joy at its feet.
Dancing fruit trees wave their hands,
While giggles burst like bubbles on lands.

Sipping dreams from a zesty cup,
The sun throws rays, like a playful pup.
Children's laughter fills the air,
As whispers of fun awaken each glare.

A tickle from vines, a splash of zest,
Sugary thoughts dance, never at rest.
Chasing shadows in the afternoon,
Sweet scents hum a light-hearted tune.

Beneath the breeze, old worries flee,
In this wacky world, oh so carefree!
The fruit is ripe, the laughter bold,
In fruity bliss, sweet tales unfold.

The Tranquil Citrus Soul

In the citrus groves, where giggles sprout,
    Each fruit reveals what joy's about.
    Whimsical birds in the trees below,
    Sing silly songs, their hearts aglow.

With each bright burst of cheerful light,
    Sour dreams spin into pure delight.
    Lemonade fountains bubbling with mirth,
    Tickle the toes of laughter's worth.

In squishy grass, playtime takes flight,
    As oranges roll like giggles at night.
    Joy spills forth, a fruitsy parade,
    With funny shapes in nature's charade.

So come along for the silly ride,
    Taste the giggles, let worries slide.
    In this tranquil realm, sweetness reigns,
    Life's zest gives way to giggly gains.

Midnight's Juicy Murmurs

Under the moon, with stars like spritz,
Midnight spreads its citrus bits.
Tangerines whisper peculiar schemes,
While sleep drapes dreams in fruity beams.

In the silliness of nighttime's glow,
A symphony of crunching, soft and slow.
With cocoa nibbles and tinkling laughs,
Dancing shadows weave silly paths.

Zesty echoes in the softest night,
Produce a giggle, pure delight.
Splashing colors, bright and bold,
Juice of wonder, warmth to hold.

When dawn arrives, fresh and new,
Tiny bursts of laughter pursue.
For what is night without playful sighs?
In juicy dreams, the fun never dies.

Clusters of Serenity and Sweetness

A grove where berries bounce with glee,
Tiny fruits share secrets, oh so free.
Jovial vines twist and tease,
While roly-poly bugs dance with ease.

In the chatter of green, joy sings high,
As sunbeams weave through leaves and sky.
Fizzy giggles bubble up like brew,
In this fruity haven, laughs break through.

Cherries chuckle, apples cheer,
Wobbling joy is always near.
On a stilting breeze, laughter will sway,
Fruity fun frames every day.

So gather round, let mischief flow,
In clusters of sweetness, spirits glow.
With every chuckle and brightened eye,
Remember: in joy, the heart will fly.

Serenities in a Citrus Garden

In a garden where laughter grows,
Citron trees wear silly clothes.
Chasing bees with wiggly feet,
Ticklish oranges say, "Hi, sweet!"

The sun winks with a cheeky grin,
While green frogs practice violin.
Spinning softly in twilight's glow,
Fruit cocktails dance, putting on a show.

Pineapple hats and grape balloon,
Squirrels sing a nutty tune.
A zesty breeze with a playful sting,
Makes each moment feel like spring!

Oh, the patch where giggles sprout,
Echoes of joy dance all about.
In this realm of flavors and cheer,
Citrus smiles bring good luck near!

Twinkling Stars in Citrus Dreams

Stars twinkle like citrus peels,
While moonlight makes the garden squeal.
Imaginary fruits take to the sky,
Juggling dreams as they bounce high.

Dancing limes and kumquat sprites,
Play hopscotch under the moonlit heights.
A tangerine tosses, smiling at me,
While oranges perch on a blush of glee.

Silly shadows prance on the floor,
Whispering secrets of fruits galore.
In this dream of whimsical hues,
Every slice tells a giggling news.

With juicy laughter in the air,
Zesty memories begin to flare.
So let's toast to the fruity delight,
Under stars that make the night bright!

The Gentle Chill of Nightfall

As nightfall wraps the garden tight,
Citrus critters prepare for flight.
Owl and grapefruit play hide and seek,
While minty chill gives him a peek.

Lemons perform a silent play,
Telling tales of a sunny day.
The moon chuckles, shining down,
On playful oranges wearing a crown.

Sipping dew from leaf to leaf,
The foliage giggles in disbelief.
Even the shadows wink with glee,
In this zesty nocturnal spree.

As breezes tickle the sleeping vines,
The garden whispers, "Oh, how it shines!"
In this gentle chill, laughter hides,
Where whimsy and sweetness coincide.

Melody of Zesty Shadows

In fields where whimsy grows so bright,
Zesty shadows dance with delight.
They twirl and leap, in crazy ways,
Singing refrains of fruity plays.

Citrus serenades in the rustling night,
Whisker-twitching tunes take flight.
The night critters join in the fun,
As Pepsi clouds race the setting sun.

With giggles hidden in every leaf,
Frolicking fruits outsmart their grief.
Sour notes blend with laughter so sweet,
Creating a tune that can't be beat.

Under starlit canopies up above,
The air is filled with citrus love.
Join the melody, let laughter flow,
In this zesty garden, let joy grow!

www.ingramcontent.com/pod-product-compliance
Lightning Source LLC
Chambersburg PA
CBHW062107280426
43661CB00086B/274